VAPOR

T0025817

Also by Sara Eliza Johnson

Bone Map

VAPOR

POEMS

SARA ELIZA JOHNSON

MILKWEED EDITIONS

Published 2022 by Milkweed Editions
Printed in the United States
Cover design by Mary Austin Speaker
Cover photo/illustration by Filippo Minelli
22 23 24 25 26 5 4 3 2 1
First Edition

Library of Congress Cataloging-in-Publication Data

Names: Johnson, Sara Eliza, author.
Title: Vapor / Sara Eliza Johnson.
Description: First Edition. | Minneapolis, Minnesota : Milkweed Editions, 2022. | Summary: "Sara Eliza Johnson's much-anticipated second collection traces human emotion and experience across a Gothic landscape of glacial and cosmic scale"-- Provided by publisher.
Identifiers: LCCN 2021052009 (print) | LCCN 2021052010 (ebook) | ISBN 9781639550586 (paperback) | ISBN 9781639550593 (ebook)
Classification: LCC PS3610.O3764 V37 2022 (print) | LCC PS3610.O3764 (ebook) | DDC 813/.6--dc23
LC record available at https://lccn.loc.gov/2021052009
LC ebook record available at https://lccn.loc.gov/2021052010

Milkweed Editions is committed to ecological stewardship. We strive to align our book production practices with this principle, and to reduce the impact of our operations in the environment. We are a member of the Green Press Initiative, a nonprofit coalition of publishers, manufacturers, and authors working to protect the world's endangered forests and conserve natural resources. *Vapor* was printed on acid-free 100% postconsumer-waste paper by McNaughton & Gunn.

CONTENTS

VAPOR

Planktonic Foraminifera

foraminifera fossils date to the earliest Cambrian era, 570 million years ago

Before microbes clustered to gleam
like the scales of alien fish

    across the back of your hand
        (your eyelashes, your lips),

before the first sunlight
wormed through the sleep behind your eyes,

before worms hollowed out the long tooth
    of the tiger in the valley

where now the milk cows
            dust their mouths
with petals and powdered bone,

            where the hearts
of the dead are bloodcrystals
rotting inside their chests,

        before there were bodies
as far as sunlight
can see, more than the light could bury,

black water covered the planet,
    and within that ocean, plankton
            glowed, constellations

that sank into the seabed,
became fossilized

                    translations for thought,
the first thought, the first
dream, for all language
you try to protect.

Written into the basalt:

cornea, follicle, fingernail
moon, wrist vein, feral bloom.

The ocean, like all oceans, tried to give the earth
a message it could not articulate
before disappearing,

a vibration you can still feel
when you press your forehead
to anything
alive or dead.

The Abyssal Zone

Sometimes it's seaweed in your throat you can't cough out
or an inkcloud expanding in your skull. Sometimes it's primal

like the force of an oyster making a pearl to protect itself
after a harvester surgically implants its poison, or the heart

growing a tumor that can't be extracted without killing you,
or pressure crushing your lungs to fists deep underwater.

Sometimes, you sink so far down from the sun your tongue
bloats like an anglerfish floating in a well, lost, unable to breathe

or speak, but each day you feel it trying to say something
about the shining dead language it once knew, watch its cells

burst into blue specks of light when you open your mouth.
A tiny syllable. Then darkness again. But each time a little bluer,

a little more like the home you've forgotten, my stranger
looking back at me from the mirror, just wanting me to reach
through and hold you.

Gravitational Wave

Alone in the field, a palpable time curves

around me, the crackling

foam of the waveform

rises and collapses

through the tiny opening

it makes inside me,

then slips through each bone like oil,

the wave a warp in my blood,

and in this field I feel the neutrino burst

inside a single cell,

before any sign of movement,

and the void contracts, grows warm again,

and my heart

stops and the sun

punctures, a black yolk spreading behind

the dustcloud,

here in the place where I

slip out into nothing

as, in a collision, a disc slips from between vertebrae

and is crushed,

there where I lose my self, reach too far toward

that sensation of belonging

I've longed for,

toward that last breath

of kindness

that passes through me,

now passing through you

Home

All the trees in the backyard have my disease,
all crooked, sad things that shake and bend
at the threat of teeth or touch, bleed sugar
and rust. I think I'm afraid to stop bleeding
because it means sleeping forever.
On one island grows a tree called *dragon's blood*
that bleeds red sap, and arthropods bleed blue
threads, the blackfin icefish bleeds clouded milk
and far south a glacier bleeds iron oxide
that still feeds an ancient ecosystem.
Even flower stems bleed latex. Everything bleeds.
Still, nothing so beautiful lives inside me,
nothing like the tenderness of horses,
their trembling eyelids and tangled manes.
Sometimes I cry in the cafe bathroom, the car,
behind a tree, so no one will see.
Sometimes I drive out to visit a stranger's horses
just to be near them, stand with them awhile
with my empty hand outstretched
like another animal, dark and small, coming out
into the light for the first time.

The Ctenophore's Transmission

a molecular clock analysis suggests that comb jellies, not the simpler sponges, are the sister group to all other animals

I have many tiny wounds
the future burns like a radioactive sap

when I open them to breathe the dark,
and many spinal cords, which scatter rainbows

in the ocean's trenches, but still the sunlight
hides from me, afraid of what can thrive

without it. I am the root curling back
into its rotted tooth, the plasma between pain

and euphoria. I am a translucent hand
feeling its way through a dark hallway forever.

The molted skin of a hand. A hand unheld
so long it atrophied and died

against the seafloor, where I'd once pressed down
to feel the heat of lava tunneling beneath it

as one day, in your curiosity, you'll press your ear
to bark and hear the sun flowing inside a tree

right before you tap it to drink
all the time and memory from it,

all rain and chlorophyll that led to this moment:
one bead of sap resting on your tongue

like a tiny, delicate moon.
Tell me, how could you want

anything more from the world
than this?

Legend

You feel dead now, but there are ways
to reach through time, to resurrect yourself.
Listen: many years ago, a reindeer died

from anthrax in the tundra. The ice kept
its body intact, and when the permafrost
melted, the carcass thawed, and the spores

awoke inside its lungs and heart, little lesions
another reindeer ate, and infected the herd,
which all died, and the shepherd boy

who tended the herd died, too,
after contaminating his whole village.
Sometimes the horrors of the world amaze me.

In laboratories, scientists have revived
bacteria frozen eight million years,
and prehistoric viruses from meltwater

which became infectious in seconds.
From this you learn we're never safe
but maybe it means we're never alone.

Under a microscope, the bacteria in me moves
like a moonfield with an amoebic flower
at its center, an ancestral organ, petaled

afterglow nothing can see, not even itself.
I know it by the fever that waxes and
wanes against my forehead, as a name

you repeat to not forget, or a word for home
when you're far away, that homesickness
when you've never been home before

but—like the miracle of the worm
regrowing its head after children cut it off—
can still somehow find your way back.

Amplituhedron

The parakeet ticks its head in all directions like a compass needle. Written in code, its feathers glow with nano-filaments, soft in my hand—the powder of alphabets. When sleeping, it tucks its head into its chest, a lemon hanging on a branch in the moonlit room. When we sleep, we tuck into each other, a puzzle box window light cracks ajar. I adore your knees: lemons full of bright wires I want to break open without breaking you.

Amplituhedron

It's spring again. We've been here before. One hummingbird pokes the eardrums of blossoms, a heartbeat pinwheeling through the air. Wind forces open a door before the rain. A dead branch blesses the roof's forehead. And there's music made of glass, which breaks into your hands. And shards that make them sing. And a bandage to stop the bleeding. And your bleeding, a diagram for flight, drawn delicately across the floor.

Amplituhedron

In our garden, the clocks tick petals away. The birdsong pulses, a severed vein, now almost empty of notes. I love all this emptiness, this warp and transparence, the whorl of atoms I brush from your brow, the ripple of brain matter in a cloud, and the virtual haze, and trembling train wires, these bees like pixels from a dream. I thought of you tender, knelt among the thorns, looking for seeds to place inside your ear for safekeeping. My infidel, before the wind tears our flesh: one more photon for your tongue.

Amplituhedron

This pain is the purest crystal, a rare love that refracts through the body in iridescent scalpels, until the organs are shot through with it. Is it surgery or execution? You cup my forehead to feel the fever's symmetry, press two fingers against my neck to find the gem that hums inside my throat like a cave full of flowers. I am choking on my own ghost. You lay me down in our bed and gently saw off my head.

Combustion

If a human has two hundred and six bones,
thirty trillion cells, and each cell
has one hundred trillion atoms, if the spine
has thirty-three vertebrae—
        if each atom
has a shadow—then the lilacs across the yard
are nebulae beginning to star.
If the fruit flies that settle on the orange
on the table rise
like the photons
                from a bomb fire miles away,
my thoughts at the moment of explosion
are nails suspended
in a jar of honey.
                    I peel the orange
for you, spread the honey on your toast.
When our skin touches
our atoms touch, their shadows
merging into a shadow galaxy.
And if echoes are shadows
of sounds, if each hexagonal cell in the body
is a dark pool of jelly,
if within each cell
drones another cell—
                The moment the bomb explodes
the man's spine bends like its shadow
across the road.
The moment he loses his hearing
I think you are calling me

from across the house
because my ears start to ring.
From the kitchen window
                I see the lilacs crackling like static
as if erasing, teleporting,
thousands of bees rising from the blossoms:
tiny flames in the sun.
I lick the knife
and the honey pierces my tongue:
                a nail made of light.
My body is wrapped in honey. When I step outside
                I become fire.

Black Hole

Six hundred and forty light years away, star is dying, shedding cells into the expanse, dragging trails of gas and dust across space the way horses drag the moon across the field with their tails. The astronomers at the observatory think they can see it: the star wheeling back, the star caving in like an eye sunk to the bottom of an ocean. There a white dot forms, the spot where everything deforms: a crushable pearl, a word plucked from a tongue. Or ripped from it, like yours. The men had held you down on the ground, cut out your tongue for a word they could not translate. Now when you open your mouth, nothing comes out but a mangled river of black sap, as if you are speaking underwater, and when your voice returns it will be as a birdcall in spring, on a planet of eyeless and earless birds.

Kwiat Paproci

fern flower

My flower on the night's forehead.
My little thunder, fetal dream
that dies before dawn.

I tasted the stain it left
on my tongue. I thought the end
of time would be a pleasure

like molten glass in my mouth,
but there is no end
to my suffering—

only another throat, another stem
to pass through like water
or blood.

Megatsunami

a sudden displacement

The wave rises like a mirror to suck the air from your lungs, inhales
all sound from city, until you can hear only the wolves, who still
call to each other in their forests beyond your vision. Or is that
the wave, creaking before collapse? Primordial oil pools in your skull
where memories float, teeth in hot tar. Soon drift the bloated horses
and beheaded sheep, cows from slaughterhouses already bled out, dead
people. Inside the wave, you crumble into a fossilized sound, like wind
trapped inside a glacier, daylight crackling away from the water
as the skin evaporates from your face, and deep within that sound,
somewhere inside you, an ancient sun touches

its first cell awake.

Fallout

When it begins to rain, we run home
with our hoods up and laughing,
muddy patches of grass

giving beneath our boots like fontanels.
I boil the water for the pasta
while you prep the chanterelles,

scrub the maps from their skullcaps
but *shhh*: a tiny sun breathes through
my palm, through the hole

in my hand (or is that your breath,
right after you've kissed it?).
I'm bleeding, washing the glow

down the sink, which swirls
like my voice in this air,
its white warp, little flame that needs

its wind to root, to flower our skin,
the field, the forest,
the whole earth

with light. And was there
a detonation of pollen, a radiant
cloud? Am I inside

out? Have I at last been
flayed, scraped clean, made
worthy of mercy?

Nebula

The anemone of your dream
blooms inside its vacuum
of black wind,

floats in radial symmetry, a remnant
of horror
uprooted from its reef.

You float

without your body, though it lingers
like a signature
of your body, of the swell and implosion

of your matter,

you a wave that reversed, curled into itself
but never
closed its loop, like sand whorling

in the desert, in that memory of violence

you still can't erase,

even now

the scorpion's tail there rippling the sand
of your mind
and the man or something in that shape
                    asking if you're all right

and you nodding yes

as he presses his hand against your neck,
between your thighs,

as the sun pulses through your palms,
                    through your chest

and how you burned open then
for your world
at its end, how your tongue

turned to blood, and your skin melted pink,
your cry for someone, or something,

                    heard across space,

like the vibrations of distant stars
instruments had once translated into sounds

for us to hear and know
it was not too late
to be alive   though it was.

Pyroclast

moves away from a volcano of up to 450 mph with temperatures up to 1,830°F.

When my body blew open
the shadowglass cloud
galloped through me, glittered

my blood to boil. Pain stretched
through its own opening,
wheezing but alive, slick

with my insides: a newborn foal
I nursed on my own milk
and licked dry after rain,

fed parts of me I could survive
without—a finger, a tooth,
the end of my tongue—

but still it tried to climb back
inside, reverse as a breath,
a scream, and still every cell

in me was a cupful
of poison dividing itself
until at its cry my skin

parted for the animal,
and, exhausted, I let it come
home. A heart can beat

outside a body. So can a wound.
Nights, it climbs out of me
to run with its kin,

trailing my blood across fields,
which yields bruises
of larkspur cows eat and die

and though I hide from it
I am relieved when it returns to sleep
in me, when I wake to feel it

breathing through my lungs
like a pool in a cave
that ripples without wind.

Hadean

At the end of this earth, a tender sound trembles through my neck, a cardinal fallen from its nest. Another tongue. The tongue in my mouth is eyeless, like the fish that lives only in caves. The one in my chest startles at its shadow, and the one in my skull hides in the coral of my brain folds, a purple leech. Many languages speak inside a body at once: particle and wave, vapor and water, sickness, eternity. I am nothing, and yet I am a body curled up on my bed, curved into the shape of a wave at the birth of a sea. The sea formed after rock vapor from the asteroid turned to rain. A moon made from the collision still floats there, like the flash of light the corpse sees in its autopsy, and on this moon, magma cools to trap water molecules in tiny stones astronauts will collect, proof there is a sea inside every thing. Mine is molten, an ancient red, and at its bottom is an exit wound that opens into another sea, immaculate and blue, that could move a dead planet to bloom.

Vapor

When it happens the rain
is not black but powder.

A noise bleeds from your ears
and everything quakes

alive inside you:
the circuits of the flowers

lighting up across a meadow,
the nanoglow

of a sea years from here
            —:And like the flash

across an event horizon,
the thought disappears

:—and then the mind threshed,
and then the brain

a perfume of proto-pollen:
a microscopic cloud

radiating in a geranium
in the meadow of another country:

a powder the elk eat
in the sudden black rain.

Vapor

Wind licks the back of your ear-bone the blown back skin
of your face.
You vaporize gasoline gleam your own blood
glowing across your hand,
your eye imploding in a powder-
light the wind drinks clean with a tongue
that was once yours,
and as the shadow welts the sky as your marrow
melts your brain turns plasma, starcore for an incandescent
moment before each cell molts
turns molten and you blue-shift,
watch from inside the shadow
your flesh become it, smear
its shape against the wall in a black sound, skeletal
as a letter when you first learned it,
your little tongue
rolling across the alphabet the way solar wind once rolled
raw matter into planets,
organs failing now in the congealed
particles you are.
Don't be afraid of it it's only the sunlight
in your sternum
carving a home for silence inside the noise
as silence had once made a soft bed for your voice to dream
its form beyond the prison of a mouth.
It was never love only annihilation a tumor, a nebula
the first shadow pressing against the back of a heart.

Vapor

The wind gallops through blood-
shot field and forest, across the cornea of water
twitching at the sudden movement of the sky.
Wind whistling the cells of what survives.
Wind the breath of blood over the skinned field
the felled trees
and in its hand a severed hand holding a smaller hand
behind which trails
a signature of blood,
and in its spit a shine of fresh cloud for your lamp,
in its ear a louse
that sings a particle no human could decipher.
But didn't the bodies burn
pearlescent? Didn't their poisoned veins
ribbon delicately around your bone-branches
and ocean trenches? Didn't their floating
mass carry all the lost flowers and flies
inside itself, a vast
meadow that bloomed a rainbowed wildfire across the waves,
radiant enough for all to feel?

Vapor

When your cells turned malignant, caved into themselves, sun poured into them, each photon an embryo returning to its egg. You vanished with it. Awake now, alone, you look out across this new planet, which bristles at your sight, having never felt an eye open and close against its skin. You are a stone cast into the shadowfield, which ripples away from you in rings. You are the needle in its muscle that sets it to twitch. You call out for help and your voice disintegrates, a sky-blue powder that contaminates each thing it touches. Call again, and the sound spikes backward into your mouth, a black liquid leaking from the holes that had just been your ears. Try again, but softer now. Trespasser, if you hope to survive here, you must forget what you are, you must be gentler, less human, like the newborn coil of light that cracks the sky's shell with its tongue.

Vapor

and then   as if up from a poisoned throat
comes this black foam of wind   this species

of wind that still smells human   of bone dust
and skin   and something breathes through

the earth again   a cell divides into another
into exoskeleton   into talons and teeth for the wild

flowers   dividing not like a body sawed
in half   but how languages meet and depart

though this world will never know itself again
will not remember the wounds it suffered here

or the fever of its infection   will have no sound
but the wind pouring dust into its own mouth

like the tongue still trying to speak
in the dust   after the men cut it out   *Please*

Migration

You are cold so I give you my skin.
We aren't hungry in dreams.
We wait for the herd to pass,
to smell their musk,
the blood that steams from gashes
in their sides, but they never come
and I cannot wake up,
the sound inside me whirring louder
now, like the black hole center,
a nail drilled
into the forehead of time.

Road to Explosion Area

I can't see anything in your dream
but a procession
of exposed spines
crawling toward a city
                    I cannot enter.
A tremor still moves
through the air, an endoskeleton
in the wind.
Paralyzed at the edge of things,
I study the grass
until white tumors
swell up like mushroom clouds
          —my eye now
a tiny cut in your dream,
opening a sky—
          I can almost see
the sound of your pain—when a cloud
settles in the sail of my lung.
Is that a breath
of sun? Is there blue? Did you
find it?

Asteroseismology

uses stars' resonances to reveal their inner structures

Like all derelict things, grief devours me.
To your eye, I seem a rotten memory,

a deformed heart decaying like a stone
after poisoned rains. I won't survive

that pain. But somewhere deep inside
me still comes a light, a molten handful

of uranium that burns a path out,
threatens to eat clean through my chest,

drain from that wound
like an infection.

Don't look then.
Turn away before the dark debrides me.

Familiar

Because they do not understand they splay me open for pleasure,

unbandage my vocal chords and I cry until they shine

like the eyes of the animal in moonlight

at the edge of the field that ran from me into the trees

before I could know it

Soon a quantum wind ropes

my neck and wrists, a wind from my mouth, my breath

tethered to the wheeling machine, my cells

turning against themselves like a garden where roots have begun

to eat the stems they grew and I am meat blossoming

in the mouth of the earth, the blood petal

between its teeth, the smoke that skins

the ground, and the black quartz

that glitters inside a bone

the lava that drips onto men's tongues

so they will never speak again

They leave me hanging

for the scavengers and when I am

transfigured, no longer human, when pain has whittled me

down into a frequency felt only by insects

like the wind through a nucleus and at last I can hear it,

the creature finds me and unfurls its skin to show me

its true face which is like my own

and licks my sores as raw light licks the swollen hills

at dawn, no longer afraid to be seen

Wormhole

structurally links separate points in spacetime, like a tunnel

Once, our forests still smelled of pine and water, so we smelled of pine and water, trout scales shining our palms for days. Now the trees stand frozen in implosion, pressing against the sky's flayed back to staunch the bleeding. But listen: hear my wrist wrinkle with a pulse, the bloodmark I make in this forest of dead things? When time here parts, another time slides through it, like a python shedding its skin, a memory of sunlight that lays itself before me in contrition, wanting love. I wrap my arms around it, lay my head against it. I put my mouth to its mouth, suck the fluid from its throat, and give it my breath, and my skin, which once was my shadow, and which can no longer feel pain. Every time it comes, it curls around me, hissing words from a language that does not yet exist, leaves blue-gleam scales on my palms, which I lick to taste, to remember the future, knowing it may be the last time, knowing all dimensions die.

Ceremony

When I arrived to this place, I felt nothing, not even the wind
on my skin. Or maybe there was no wind here, or maybe no skin.
But then I felt curious. And then came a tingling in my throat
and then I was crying, though I didn't know why,
and then tender, like a fawn that walks toward a stranger's hand
full of grass, after it has known hunger, but before it's been hunted
and this I'd recognized as the beginning of desire, and then
I knew my need for touch exceeded my fear, and it was time
to go. I can't hide in this cloud any longer, so afraid of living.
I must be careful, but not hesitate, having learned panic trembles
a surgeon's hand to slaughter, that the space between mercy
and mutilation is the second between the blade and the neck.
First, I slice the scar on my chest, the one so old I renamed it
many times, as if a child of my own. Next, I turn up my hand
to catch what slides from its opening: a single yolk, miraculously still
intact, like a memory congealed inside me. Then I break
it on my tongue, knowing to swallow quick, no matter how
sour or sick the taste, how rotten I've become inside,
though I didn't expect it to burn going down, that it would hurt
more than any wound that had sent me here to hide.
When the pain comes, I remind myself this is what I wanted
in the end: to remember how to be human
again, to feel with my whole body, not despite the pain
but because of it.

Coma

Alive means waking
from one dream
into another. In this

I lick the wound
to taste myself,
which is the void between stars

turned cellular,
the sinewed note
of a vacuum that bleeds

into anyone
who puts their mouth
to its sound.

My body opens elsewhere
and elsewhere, until
I forget. And forget

what I am. The hardest part
of being alive is
some hungers

are infinite. This one
is like the last sunlight
sneaking through before

the eye closes again, a piece
of the world I left
and cannot surrender.

There is always a sliver
in my tongue
I cannot pant out.

Terra Incognita

Out here, I'm lonely enough to open
my body for anyone that finds me,

hoping they'll anoint me
like a primordial light loosed

from a fossil, a wind trapped in ice
for four million years. I wait here

to be seen. When you reach me,
you slit me from neck to groin

as if peeling a fruit
you have just discovered, my pain

a pearlin nectar trickling
into your cupped hands

like an extraterrestrial spring.
You have never been hurt.

Never been cut, been sacrament.
I dare you: put your mouth

to the wound you've made of me
and breathe in.

Titan

Ligeia Mare

In the shadowlake
under the lake, in the zone
of your skeleton

a tremor flowers:
a cell blooms:
nucleoplasm spreading

like a submerged moon.
Then acetylene flashes
its nuclear eye,

and soon you breathe
in this mirror:
though not whole,

your thought has found
a shape. A wave
erupts beneath you,

through your plasma
like a voice in static,
and you float

to the surface
where you release
your wound: the island

that one day someone
will probe for life, try
to decipher. The lake

ripples against you
and, grateful to be touched,
you ripple back.

Titan

Kraken Mare

As a storm forms above the lake, capillary waves open across it, and soon
a wind spirals the vapor into rain, and then rain and hail
slit the waves
into waves,

like the desert wind that had once slept beneath the eyelids
of your corpse, had rippled them open,
before the fire ants could eat them,

as a wind had once disemboweled you, hollowed out your face so that light
pooled into your skull,
as water into a cave.

Now you open your new eyes in this lake—
or not your eyes but a memory
of sight—as like blood vessels the waves open in you—

and the warmth settles back into you, as you remember the sun on your face
and how someone had laughed and taken your hands, and in some other
moment the weight of the sun and the blood vessel burst in your eye
from crying

—you the brightest mote in the eye of the lake
that opens for you, lets you
grow your mind deeper within it, and which through you learns the miracle
of mitosis: a kind of breathing through dream.

Titan

Jingpo Lacus

This lake holds you as if it knows
your form, has felt you before.

Like a wave circling back,
your body steps through itself

as you step through the lake
and your skin opens to let the ultraviolet

light inside, and a crystal
seeds, and more crystals grow,

until your spine is a reef
and your heart bleeds out

a new species of darkness
to populate its glow.

The lake is an iris, and you
are its pupil dilating to eclipse

the blue, your blood cells
microscopic black stars

that breed below its shining.
You rise from it like a cloud

of oil, a reflection
climbing from its mirror

or the pain from the wound
or the trauma

from an eye—this break
between the break

from which a strange tenderness
begins to flood.

Exoplanet TrES-2b

reflects less than one percent of the sunlight falling on it

Here blood flows through the field
in fine threads
and a black dew whirs
against your face
across your neck,
behind your eyelids,
a creature reading your scent.
You press against its fur
trying also to understand,
brace for pain,
having always known yourself
as the tumor of any valley or breast
to be crushed or cut
away. But this power is tender,
the opposite of machine.
It is the blur
tucked behind the lung
on the X-ray, hides
from all but you, washes you
from the inside,
as a sea swarms through the moon
its honey.

Exoplanet HD 189733b

has blue color that likely comes from a rain of molten glass, with winds seven times the speed of sound

Your love is a blue wind,
the skin of suffocation.

A lung imploding
like a beehive.

A wind that moves
in all dimensions, pulls

veins through the wrist
in glittering loops,

mercury loosed
from a thermometer,

and I would drink it
for one more second here,

I would place my head
on the altar.

Exoplanet Proxima Centauri b

is subject to stellar wind pressures of more than 2,000 times those of Earth

When the flare reaches this desert, falls as radioactive
pollen across the sand, the bees come curious.
They take granules one by one to the hive,
to the sky they will build underground, and soon
they vibrate, dream together; for the first time
they realize they are thinking together.
An ultraviolet virus, they press up against the ground
like a fever about to burst
a mind open, a gem heated to shatter
and then shatter to make a new spring, where sky
sprouts from dirt, where you wake one day, many years
after the earth has died, and find yourself,
an alien thought walking the fields, your bare feet
pressing each flower out.

Migration

Light foams around my mouth
like spit around a horse's mouth

I am a translucent lung inhaling
and exhaling

I am a sunlight that stretches
to hold everything

inside it like a chrysanthemum
like the love once promised me

and my skeleton creaks open
but he never comes

only the emaciated animals
the wretched and abandoned

creatures that climb inside me
to be warm

to eat the apples of my breasts
drink from my spine

as one day I will come to myself
limping and starved

Revelation

I am ready to be loved by any thing.
For your love, I'd wash your feet, bake you bread,
water your flowers when you're away.

I'd sleep outside with them, would pour
blood straight from my wrist to feed them.
I'd cut the circle in my chest to make space

for the moon, let a star nest inside me
like a scorpion, just to feel its love
though it would hurt. And though it would hurt,

if I could not be loved, I'd puncture my skull
through the ear and drip every dream
I've had into the soil, a shadowhoney

for the worms to eat, if they might know me
as one of them, teach me how to move
through their darkness. I'd feed my heart

to a snake if it would show me how to change
skins, how to survive as an unloveable thing.
I would cut my soul out to make room

for another soul, push it out in loops
the way frostflowers, in those first hours
of spring, push through the stems in a field,

mimicking flowers. I'd push through myself
the way pain had pushed through my brain,
like a tooth through a gum, until I could

no longer contain it. Stranger, I'd even lie
down for the axe if it could make me new.
In my mind, the moment is so beautiful:

my head will roll away from my neck
like the shadow through the eclipse,
like a stone from the door of a tomb.

Then I'll climb out of that body, a lamb
with claws and a sleeping viper
where a beating heart should be, lamb

that could kill if you came any closer,
lamb that eats the wildflowers
from your hand without fear.

Lazarus

Through the mist I see as the first mammals
once saw through their forests, dark photons
translating matter into shape:
shadowflower, shadowstone, the ripple
of bees and their shadowblood weeping
inside the trees. My first eye stares back at mine
and into my chest pours a weight, an infinite
pressure inside my heart or left lung
like an extinction echoing backward
into the first cell of its animal,
my body colder in that spot.
A thumbprint blooms between my breasts
where a stranger once pressed
and being so alone
I open like a grave.

Mutant

All the wildflowers turn away from me
as I pull my shame up from my throat,
hold it up to sunlight to inspect its anatomy.
See how this organ labors to breathe in my palm,
a black jellyfish, a tentacled heart still
connected to me by a single blue vein?
I know everything needs love, even this creature
which opens, despite its pain, to show me
its insides, a secret I cannot tell you
because I also have a secret. Sometimes I pin
my hair up to expose my neck to the breeze,
release it in a cloud when I hear you coming.
Sometimes I cover my skin when I feel your eyes
as if I might turn inside out. I am the dream
with a mind but no mouth. Or a mouth
with dreams, but no tongue. Or I'm a tongue
skinned from speaking, which is like a corpse
in the process of blooming a tree that will hide it
for centuries. If only I could let you inside
my mouth, you'd understand why it's so hard
for me to speak. Even my kisses turn
to blisters. If I let you inside you'll never find
your way out. Some desires can't live outside water
or wombs. Some words crumble outside the mouth
like bone fragments unearthed in disaster.
Let me explain. Deep within a nuclear power plant
where many men died saving their city
a mass of black corium swells inside
a concrete sarcophagus. One day, its radiation

will leak back out into the land, no matter how
many times they try to reseal its tomb.
They call this substance *the elephant's foot*
and say its skin looks like tree bark,
but even now it burns a poison light
only the dead can see, and this is like me:
I am an irradiated thing that needs someone
to hold it closed, and no one can hold a thing
like that long enough to love it
unless maybe they, too, have been ruined,
cast out or kept hidden,
named *abomination*
after someone tried to bury their power
and failed.

Polydipsia

As a servant of thirst,
I've walked my feet skinless
to find this tiny jewel
the glacier kept whole and cold
as if for my mouth alone: a lost
memory that pushes like a tooth
through my tongue
so I can taste it forever:
how pure your love felt
before it severed me
clean from this world,
Amen.

Migration

We shadows return to the trees, scraping the ground
like a snake shedding its skin, or a wolf licking
a chest cavity, or your teeth against my neck
in the dream I can't stop having, though I move
with the herd now, an alphabet growing
under my skin, wind tracing each letter
with its tongue, learning its form. *Who erased*
your face? the wind asks. *How do you see*
without eyes? If I could answer I would say
I see as nectar tunneling through a moon.
Not through glass, but as dark that learns to love itself,
as cloud tissue, as the black glue that holds
each thing together, though light would separate it.
I see as the tiny ripple that moves through muscle
before an earthquake or massacre, the word
opening its lesion, the blood of the martyr
as it exits the wrist. I see through the hole in my chest
that breathes as black holes had breathed
against the eyes of the astronomers.
When I reach the forest, the trees are soft enough
to push a hand through. I find mine among them
and, ready to begin the long work of growing
away from the sunlight that still laps its memory
at the edge of my mind, I break my spine, fold
my body inside, and become paradise.

Geode

You remember: the moon over the city
had been eaten by worms.
You remember how it had no face,

how the windows were iced honeycombs
as your mother left the church
with a basket of cured meat and eggs and bread

covered with a handkerchief,
your mother walking and her shadow,
your mother her body at night a plot of dirt

and her blue eyes the first flowers the wind
permits, and ahead a white horse
plodding its carriage past soldiers

with machine guns—the *scrape, scrape*
of horseshoes on stone—and the wind-
warp of a train, and the snow swell through an alley

like blood rushing into a brain cavity.
Think of all this. How each skull,
like a geode, holds a crystal colony inside:

a glittering of synapse, quartz-
glints of dreams you have not had, mirror-
bits of other faces and cities you know

because someone has told you them.
Any bullet there could have been hers.
Any one could have made a hole

in her head. Then crystals would have bled
into the air, onto the wind
like the snow wafting into the house

through the window you forgot to close
which is why, you realize,
you are shivering.

NOTES

"Black Hole" is written after Stephen Hawking's statement in his 2005 paper "Information Loss in Black Holes," first published in *Physics Review,* that "If you jump into a black hole, your mass energy will be returned to our universe, but in a mangled form which contains the information about what you were like but in a state where it can not be easily recognized. It is like burning an encyclopedia. Information is not lost, if one keeps the smoke and the ashes. But it is difficult to read."

"Road to Explosion Area" is written after a photo of the same title, dated April 18, 1947 and located in the Texas City Disaster Photographs collection in Special Collections at the University of Houston Libraries.

"Kwiat Paproci" is the Polish term for the fern flower, a magical flower in Baltic mythology that blooms instantaneously—with a crack like thunder—for a brief moment on the summer solstice. The flower brings good fortune and power, but often at a price, and is guarded by mythological creatures.

The "Amplituhedron" poems are titled after the mathematical concept proposed by Nima Arkani-Hamed and Jaroslav Trnka. Most of my understanding of the concept stems from the Natalie Wolchover's 2013 article "A Jewel at the Heart of Quantum Physics" in *Quanta Magazine,* in which she describes it as "a jewel-like geometric object that dramatically simplifies calculations of particle interactions and challenges the notion that space and time are fundamental components of reality."

The "Titan" poems are written after the methane lakes of Titan, one of Saturn's moons.

"Exoplanet Proxima Centauri b" takes its inspiration from the article "Bees learn while they sleep, and that means they might dream" by Alex Riley, published on August 25, 2016 at BBC.com.

"Lazarus" is loosely inspired by a statement on dark photons by Sergei Gninenko, as quoted in the article "NA64 hunts the mysterious dark photon" at CERN's website: "To use a metaphor, an otherwise impossible dialogue between two people not speaking the same language (visible and dark matter) can be enabled by a mediator (the dark photon), who understands one language and speaks the other one."

ACKNOWLEDGMENTS

My gratitude to the editors of the following publications in which these poems, sometimes in earlier versions, appeared:

Academy of American Poets: "Combustion," "Vapor" (1)
Alaska Quarterly Review: "Home," "Legend"
Birdfeast: "Vapor" (4), "Vapor" (5)
Blackbird: "Asteroseismology," "Lazarus," "Wormhole"
Cincinnati Review: "Vapor" (2)
Colorado Review: "Polydipsia"
Copper Nickel: "Titan (I)," "Titan (II)," "Titan (III)"
Crazyhorse: "Familiar"
descant: "Black Hole," "Fallout," "Planktonic Foraminifera"
February, an Anthology: "Vapor" (3)
Gulf Coast: "Road to Explosion Area"
Grist: "Megatsunami"
New England Review: "Migration" (3)
North Dakota Review: "Amplituhedron" (1), "Amplituhedron" (2), "Amplituhedron" (3)
Queen Mob's Tea House: "Exoplanet Tres-2b," "Exoplanet Proxima Centauri b"
Rock & Sling: "Hadean," "Migration (II)"
Salt Hill: "Geode"
Southern Indiana Review: "Mutant," "Revelation"
Virginia Quarterly Review: "Gravitational Wave," "Nebula," "Pyroclast," "Terra Incognita," "The Abyssal Zone"

Many thanks to the National Endowment for the Arts, the University of Utah Creative Writing Program, the Fine Arts Work Center in Provincetown, the Virginia Center for the Creative Arts, and the Taft-Nicholson Center Environmental Humanities Center, whose support made this book possible.

Thank you to the crew at Milkweed Editions for all their careful attention, labor, and effort spent making this book a reality.

I'm forever grateful to Susannah Nevison, Rebecca Lindenberg, Margaret Reges, Claire Wahmanholm, Laura Bylenok, Emilia Phillips, Sumita Chakraborty, Rachel Mennies, Tessa Fontaine, Joe Sacksteder, and other trusted friends who read work from this manuscript over the years, and helped it grow into a book.

Thanks also to professors Katharine Coles, Paisley Rekdal, and Jacqueline Osherow for their guidance.

And thank you to my parents, for being there and supporting me, always and without reservation.

SARA ELIZA JOHNSON is the author of *Vapor* and *Bone Map,* which was a winner of the 2013 National Poetry Series. Her poetry has appeared in the *Virginia Quarterly Review, Colorado Review, New England Review, Boston Review, Copper Nickel, Ninth Letter, Blackbird, Crazyhorse, Pleiades,* the Best New Poets series, *Salt Hill, Cincinnati Review,* and the Academy of American Poets Poem-A-Day program, among other venues. She is the recipient of a National Endowment for the Arts Fellowship, a Rona Jaffe Foundation Writers' Award, two Winter Fellowships from the Fine Arts Work Center in Provincetown, and a residency from the Virginia Center for the Creative Arts. Johnson is an assistant professor at the University of Alaska, Fairbanks.

Founded as a nonprofit organization in 1980, Milkweed Editions is an independent publisher. Our mission is to identify, nurture and publish transformative literature, and build an engaged community around it.

Milkweed Editions is based in Bdé Óta Othúŋwe (Minneapolis) within Mní Sota Makhóčhe, the traditional homeland of the Dakhóta people. Residing here since time immemorial, Dakhóta people still call Mní Sota Makhóčhe home, with four federally recognized Dakhóta nations and many more Dakhóta people residing in what is now the state of Minnesota. Due to continued legacies of colonization, genocide, and forced removal, generations of Dakhóta people remain disenfranchised from their traditional homeland. Presently, Mní Sota Makhóčhe has become a refuge and home for many Indigenous nations and peoples, including seven federally recognized Ojibwe nations. We humbly encourage our readers to reflect upon the historical legacies held in the lands they occupy.

milkweed.org

Milkweed Editions also gratefully acknowledges sustaining support from our Board of Directors; the Alan B. Slifka Foundation and its president, Riva Ariella Ritvo-Slifka; the Amazon Literary Partnership; the Ballard Spahr Foundation; *Copper Nickel*; the McKnight Foundation; the National Endowment for the Arts; the National Poetry Series; the Target Foundation; and other generous contributions from foundations, corporations, and individuals. Also, this activity is made possible by the voters of Minnesota through a Minnesota State Arts Board Operating Support grant, thanks to a legislative appropriation from the arts and cultural heritage fund. For a full listing of Milkweed Editions supporters, please visit milkweed.org.

Interior design by Tijqua Daiker
Typeset in Arno

Arno was designed by Robert Slimbach. Slimbach named this typeface after the river that runs through Florence, Italy. Arno draws inspiration from a variety of typefaces created during the Italian Renaissance; its italics were inspired by the calligraphy and printing of Ludovico degli Arrighi.